ABOUT THE AUTHOR

Nick James has been an aquarist since his early days at school. Growing up in Rhodesia (now Zimbabwe), he was an avid angler and spent most holidays on Lake Kariba on the Zambesi river. It was here that his love of cichlids took root.

He has an MSc degree in ichthyology, and has worked as a research officer at the world-renowned JLB Smith Institute of Ichthyology.

Christened 'Nichlid' for his love of rearing cichlids, he now runs his own cichlid hatchery on his farm near Grahamstown (Eastern Cape, South Africa). He shares his home with his wife and three young daughters, and breeds nearly 100 different species of cichlids for sale to the aquarium trade.

Photography: Nick James (pages 4, 11, 13, 32, 33, 34, 37, 39, 40, 42, 45, 48, 50, 51, 54, 57, 59), Ian Watson (page 6), Mary Bailey (page 17), Keith Allison, and courtesy of Tetra UK, and Interpet.
Picture editor: Claire Horton-Bussey
Design: Rob Benson

Published by Ringpress Books,
a division of Interpet Publishing,
Vincent Lane, Dorking, Surrey, RH4 3YX, UK
Tel: 01306 873822   Fax: 01306 876712
email: sales@interpet.co.uk

First published 2002
© 2002 Ringpress Books. All rights reserved

ISBN 1 86054 276 X

Printed and bound in Hong Kong through
Printworks International Ltd.

10 9 8 7 6 5 4 3 2 1

CONTENTS

WHAT IS A LAKE VICTORIA CICHLID?

Cichlids (family Cichlidae) are perciform (perch-like) fish native to Africa, tropical America, Madagascar, the Middle East, and parts of the Indian subcontinent. Their distant ancestors probably lived in the sea, but today, although they have marine 'cousins', they are restricted to fresh and brackish water.

No single feature distinguishes cichlids from other fish, but all have a single pair of nostrils, and spines in the dorsal, anal and pelvic fins. Most have an interrupted (two-part) lateral line (a row of sensory pores along each flank, sensitive to vibration, used to detect nearby objects, prey, and predators, for example).

Haplochromis is the main genus of Lake Victoria cichlid that is kept in aquaria. Pictured: adult male *Haplochromis chilotes* in breeding colorati◄

Lake Victoria cichlids are less well known among fishkeepers than Lake Malawi species, such as the *Nimbochromis livingstoni*, pictured.

All cichlids are egg-layers and practise a high degree of parental care. Their breeding strategies are variable: e.g. some brood eggs and/or fry in their mouths, others (substrate-spawners) attach eggs to a surface, and guard them and the resulting fry.

AFRICAN CICHLIDS

African cichlids fall into two main groups on the basis of ancestry, the tilapiine and the haplochromine lineages (there are other, smaller groups as well). Both groups contain large species important as foodfish for humans, and smaller ones often ideally suited to aquarium maintenance.

Haplochromine cichlids have evolved 'species flocks' (groups of closely related species) in some East African lakes, including Lake Victoria. These 'haps' are often small, brightly coloured, interesting in their behaviour, and, if properly managed, hardy and long-lived (five to ten years) in the aquarium; most are also easy to breed in captivity.

LAKE VICTORIA

Most aquarists who keep cichlids are familiar with the fish from the East African Rift Valley Lakes (lakes Malawi and Tanganyika), but, until comparatively recently, Lake Victoria has remained rather a less well-known area of fishkeeping.

Decades of political unrest and inaccessibility are the chief reasons for this, rather than the fish themselves, as Lake Victoria holds a wealth of beautiful and interesting cichlids suitable for aquaria.

This book is intended to give a brief guide to the pitfalls and possibilities of keeping these cichlids in the home aquarium.

Lake Victoria has many sloping shores with beaches and marshy areas, but also has rocky headlands.

CICHLIDS FROM AROUND THE WORLD

Heros efasciatus (South America).

Paretroplus maculatus (Madagascar).

Melanochromis auratus (Lake Malawi).

The Lake Victorian basin contains many satellite lakes, including Lake George. Pictured: *Astatoreochromis alluaudi*, from the Lake Victoria and Lake George basins.

ORIGINS AND GEOGRAPHY

Lake Victoria straddles the Equator, and like the East African Rift Valley, supports a rich tropical fish fauna. Unlike Lakes Malawi and Tanganyika, it is not a rift valley lake, and has a maximum depth of only 100 metres (328 ft), with much of the lake only 10 to 15 metres (approximately 33 ft) deep.

Whereas the rift lakes have steep rocky shores, in places plunging to great depths underwater (down to more than 1,000 m/3280 ft in the case of Lake Tanganyika), Lake Victoria has mostly gently sloping shores with beaches and marshy areas. There are, however, rocky headlands and islands that greatly resemble parts of the Lake Malawi coastline, and it is from these areas that most of the Victorian cichlids kept in aquaria originate.

The Lake Victoria basin includes numerous smaller 'satellite' lakes and swamps such as the Yala swamp and Lake Kanyaboli in the east; Lake Kyoga and Lake

Nawampasa to the north on the Victoria Nile, now isolated from Lake Victoria itself by the Owen Falls (dammed in the 1950s). In the west, Lakes Edward and George are connected to Lake Victoria through the Katonga River, an ephemeral vegetation-choked channel that may now be a barrier to fish movements, but was open water during wetter times.

> **MBUNA AND MBIPI**
> Whereas rock-dwellers from Lake Malawi are known collectively as 'mbuna', those from Lake Victoria are called 'mbipi'.

CLINGING TO SURVIVAL

Over the millennia more than 350 species of small haplochromine cichlids evolved in Lake Victoria. Then, during the 1950s, the Ugandan authorities stocked the lake with the Nile perch (*Lates niloticus*), a predatory foodfish from the lower Nile river.

For many years there were few signs of changes in the fish fauna. But with massively increasing human population growth during the 1960s and 1970s the lake came under pressure from fertiliser pollution and erosion of the catchment through overgrazing and agriculture. This has resulted in a massively increased inflow of nutrients and silt into the formerly clear waters of Lake Victoria.

Suddenly the balance was upset: the clear waters of the lake became murky with algae blooms; the Nile perch population exploded and preyed heavily on the small cichlids, rapidly decimating their numbers.

Other exotic cichlids such as *Oreochromis niloticus*,

introduced for the commercial food-fisheries, also rapidly increased their numbers at the expense of the indigenous species flock. The result of this disaster was the virtual extinction of many open water haplochromine species. Only the rock-dwelling species managed to survive due to the shelter provided by their natural habitat.

As a result of this mass near extinction, scientists suddenly became aware of the disaster happening before their eyes and considerable research took place on the lake during the late 1980s and 90s. Imports of many Lake Victoria cichlid species were brought into Europe and the USA, and both hobbyists and conservationists alike gained first-hand experience of these unfamilar cichlids. As a consequence of this intense interest, many new species were discovered, and the popularity of these cichlids grew.

POST-*LATES*

The findings of many studies carried out since the Nile perch 'boom' have shown that numerous formerly numerically abundant species are now virtually extinct in Lake Victoria itself.

However, in some of the satellite water bodies, closely related, or even 'relict' species have been discovered, which are now absent from Lake Victoria itself. These are species that may have formerly populated the entire Lake Victoria basin, including what is now the main lake itself, but which are now limited to isolated populations, perhaps due to various factors such as inability to evolve with changing conditions, failure to compete with other more successful species, and stressful climatic changes.

Astatotilapia latifasciata from Lake Nawampasa would be highly vulnerable to Nile perch, at present absent from this small lake.

Examples are *Haplochromis phytophagus* from the Yala swamp, and *Astatotilapia latifasciata* from Lake Nawampasa (a small lake on the fringes of, but isolated from, Lake Kyoga, which itself has an indigenous population of Nile perch).

Other lesser-known species come from nearby Lake George (e.g. *H.* sp. 'emerald fire') and Lake Edward (*H. aeneocolor*).

SCIENTIFIC AND COMMON NAMES

Many aquarists are confused by the lack of common names, and the inconsistent scientific names often used for Lake Victoria cichlids.

In 1980, top ichthyologist Dr. Humphry Greenwood split the Victoria haplochromines into numerous genera, but his work did not gain universal acceptance, and many scientists and aquarists have reverted to the use of *Haplochromis* for them all, sometimes using Greenwood's nomina in parentheses, e.g. *Haplochromis (Ptyochromis) sauvagei*.

Greenwood's genera are still used in some quarters and *Astatotilapia* seems to be generally accepted, e.g.

Astatotilapia nubila. However, many wholesalers and retailers still use the old name *Haplochromis nubilus*, and the hobbyist is left wondering if they really are the same species!

Numerous species remain scientifically undescribed and have informal names that reflect details of place names where the species was first collected (e.g. *H.* sp. 'Hippo Point'), their colour or other distinguishing aspects (e.g. *H.* sp. 'velvet black'), or even perceived similarities with other well-known fish species (e.g. *H.* sp. 'rock kribensis').

The process by which a species is scientifically described can be a long one, and involves in-depth research into related species, detailed morphological examination, and, preferably, study of behavioural aspects, such as breeding and feeding. Once all this information has been published, it has to undergo peer review, which may result in either acceptance or rejection of the suggested name by the scientific community.

Mutiply this process by the several hundred cichlid species known to occur in the lake, with distinct 'species complexes' of very closely-related cichlids, sometimes extending over a wide geographical area. Then complicate the procedure with logistical factors, such as difficult access and political unrest. The result is a recipe that sends most taxonomists scuttling for easier work!

CONFUSING COMMON NAMES

On a practical note, it is better to avoid giving Lake Victoria haplochromine cichlids 'common names'. It only causes confusion, and the potential mixing up of

Cichlids are often named after their distinguishing features. *Haplochromis* sp. 'Rock Kribensis' (pictured) is so-called because of its perceived similarity to the 'kribensis' (*Pelvicachromis pulcher*) of West Africa.

species can – and does – lead to the hybridisation of closely-related species by aquarists unaware of the taxonomic differences. The pseudo-scientific names given to these fish by the *Haplochromis* Ecology Survey Team at the University of Leiden, Holland – for example, *H.* sp. 'red head nyererei' – are quite adequate for the moment until the distinct species are scientifically described.

To illustrate the type of confusion that abounds with common names or descriptions, I am often asked if I keep "that blue-striped Malawi cichlid?" To which I always reply, "which of the 100-or-so blue-striped Malawi species do you mean?" A little pompous, but it has the desired effect of making the questioner realise that Nature is a lot more creative than his experience would lead him to believe!

CHAPTER 2

CHOOSING THE RIGHT CICHLIDS

While Lake Victoria has more than 300 species of small cichlids suitable for aquaria, many of these have only slight taxonomic differences that the average aquarist would not be aware of.

There are around 35-50 regularly traded species which are captive bred and appear on wholesalers' lists. Most of these are the brightly coloured rock-dwelling species from Lake Victoria itself, or species from peripheral swamps and lakes in the main lake basin.

NUTRITIONAL COMPATIBILITY

Most of the species sold are compatible as their individual ecological niches are very similar. They are largely feeders on algae and aquatic insects or snails from rocks covered with aufwuchs, the thick algal mat which encrusts rocks.

Aufwuchs harbours numerous invertebrates and other micro-organisms that serve as food to grazing fish. Some species consume the invertebrates as a by-product of eating the algae, while others pick out the tiny edible organisms with jaws especially evolved for this purpose.

There are a few more predatory or piscivorous species, such as *H.* sp. 'matumbi hunter' and *H.* sp. 'orange rock hunter', that are regularly offered for sale, and whilst these may be compatible with the former types in an aquarium, they will require a higher protein

diet than the vegetarian species in order to flourish and
show full colour.

BUYER BEWARE

Aquarists may be confused by the availability of
differing species with similar names: e.g. *H*. sp. 'red
head nyererei' from Zue Island or *H*. sp. 'red flank
nyererei' from Nansio Island. These names identify the
particular species from the 23 or so other members of
the *H. nyererei* species complex that are found around
the lake.

Fish sold by any retailer simply as '*Haplochromis
nyererei*' can be assumed to be highly suspect, if no
other information on origin is available, and are most
probably hybrids of little value.

Beware of fish labelled 'mixed Victorians', as you will not be sure of
what you are getting. All fish should be clearly identified.

COMMON SPECIES NAMES

Victorian and other non-rift-lake haplochromines commonly available from wholesalers/retailers or hobbyist breeders in Europe and the USA

Species	Accepted common or trade name
Astatotilapia piceata	*Astatotilapia piceata*
A. nubila	*Haplochromis nubilus*
A. latifasciata	
(Lake Nawampasa)	*Zebra obliquidens*
Haplochromis argens	
H. chilotes	Thick lips
H. sp. 'copperblack'	
H. sp. 'crimson tide'	
H. sp. 'deepwater'	
H. sp. 'fire red'	
H. sp. 'flameback'	Flameback
H. sp. 'emerald fire'	
(Lake George)	Emerald fire
H. limax	
H. sp. 'matumbi hunter'	
H. nyererei	
H. sp. 'rock kribensis'	Rock kribensis
H. phytophagus	
(Yala swamp)	Christmas Fulu
H. sp. 'red tail sheller'	
H. sp. 'thick skin'	*H. obliquidens,* H. sp. 44
H. sp. 'migori'	Migori
H. sp. 'velvet black'	
H. sauvagei	

The best dealers will provide the right décor so the fish feel safe and secure, and show their best colours.

If your retailer marks his Victorians simply as 'mixed Victorians', then you can be sure that he does not know his trade – buy elsewhere! Such dealers almost invariably mix species together with the assurance that they can tell the difference between the females.

The best shops keep different species of Victorians in separate tanks, marked with the correct species name and its geographic origin. If they have taken this much trouble, they deserve your support, and you can be more confident that the fish are really what they are advertised to be!

CHAPTER
3

CREATING A HOME

Collecting wild-caught Victoria cichlids is a hit-and-miss activity. The lake is immense (300 kms/186 miles across!), the infrastructure primitive in terms of transport, accommodation, and other essential facilities, and the desirable species are scattered over a wide area. This makes the logistics of catching, holding and dispatching very expensive.

For these reasons, most Victorian cichlids available today are captive-bred in Europe, South Africa and the USA. Luckily, most species are easy to breed and captive-bred stocks are usually of good quality.

On the down side, many Victorian cichlid species will interbreed (hybridise) readily under captive conditions, and great care has to be taken to keep species separate to prevent this.

Some Asian-bred stocks have been shown to be suspect in this regard, and the well-known 'Haplochromis nubilus' (correct name: Astatotilapia nubila) offered from the Far East is likely to be a hybrid of several different species all with the common black-with-red-fins coloration seen in many Victorian cichlids.

Aquarists should beware of such suspect stock! Furthermore, correct identification of founder stock is difficult as so few species have been scientifically described.

Malawi mbuna (pictured) are often too aggressive for Lake Victoria cichlids, so generally the two types should not be kept together.

MIXING AND MATCHING

Lake Victoria cichlids are best kept by themselves. Numerous people ask if they can keep Victorians with Malawis or Tanganyikans: the answer, generally, is 'no', with a few exceptions.

The Tanganyikan cichlids generally require much harder water than the Victorians, and the smaller species of such genera as *Julidochromis* tend to be dominated by their more rumbustious behaviour.

Conversely, Malawi mbuna (the rock-dwelling species) are sometimes too aggressive for Victorians and dominate them so that their colours are suppressed and breeding activity does not take place.

Many Victorian cichlids tend to be more 'mellow' than their Lake Malawi cousins. Indeed, with certain species, even aquarium plants will survive undisturbed if adequate alternative cover is supplied in terms of rocks, driftwood or caves – many other cichlid species 'vandalise' plants, much to the annoyance of their owners.

However, it is a matter of personal choice whether you decide to keep species from the different East African lakes together. There are no hard-and-fast rules, except that the temperament of the differing species must match, and they must share the same environmental requirements in terms of water quality, space or shelter.

If you want to breed Lake Victoria cichlids, then keep only one species per tank to prevent possible hybridisation, or two species that look dramatically different.

I often feel that people who want to mix either Victorian, Malawi or Tanganyika cichlids with all the other community tank fish available are somewhat akin to those who would put fancy wheels and go-faster stripes on a Mercedes! It does not look right, nor does it work well.

One possible exception to this is the addition of some small *Synodontis* catfish, for example *S. nyassae*, *S. petricola*, or *S. multipunctatus*, which are not out of place in a Lake Victoria cichlid aquarium.

Avoid potentially large sucker-mouth (loricariid) type catfishes, such as *Hypostomus plecostomus*, as they will compete with your cichlids for food (algae on the rocks), and most certainly avoid *Pangasius*, which can grow much too large.

Some of the smaller South American catfish are carnivorous or omnivorous, but remember that most require softwater conditions to thrive. Dwarf catfish from South America (*Corydoras*, *Hoplosternum* and smaller loricariid catfishes) may survive well enough, but, in my opinion, look totally wrong in a Lake Victoria aquarium, and ruin the overall impression that has been created.

Large catfish, such as the *Glyptoperichthys gibbiceps* (above) will compete with the cichlids for food so are unsuitable as tank-mates.

WATER CONDITIONS

The parameters of the water conditions required by Lake Victoria cichlids can all be measured quite adequately by using the test kits available from most aquarist stores.

Water parameters should include a neutral to mildly alkaline pH (7-8), although most species are quite forgiving regarding alkalinity. The hardness (calcium/magnesium content) can also vary from slightly to moderately hard 6-10 dGH (degrees of German hardness). A conductivity of 150-300 microsiemens is ideal.

Aquarium temperature should be within the range 23 to 28 degrees C (73 to 82 degrees F). Captive fish appear to live longer at the lower end of the temperature range but the higher levels are needed for breeding.

As with all tropical fish species in captivity, filtration must be first class. Undergravel filters are not recommended, except with the addition of a 'gravel tidy' (plastic grid buried in the gravel to prevent the under-gravel plate from being exposed by digging). The best filtration is that provided by external canister or 'hang-on' type filters.

Where the tap water is soft, it is highly recommended that crushed shell is either included as part of the filter medium (preferably) or as part of the substratum, mixed with coarse sand of 3-4 mm (0.15 inch) grain size. This buffers the pH from falling excessively into the acidic range, and, as it works on a 'slow-release' basis, is long lasting.

TANK DÉCOR

Gravel should be dark in colour, especially for the more timid species as this gives them some sense of security, especially with bright lighting. A male *Haplochromis* sp. 'flameback' will look very washed out if it is brightly illuminated over white gravel, but regains its scarlet dorsal and gold flanks over dark gravel, provided other conditions are right.

Tough plants, such as *Vallisneria*, which have substantial roots, are ideal for a Victorian tank. Hard rocks, such as slate or quartzite, can be piled up to form caves and hide-aways.

Well-cured driftwood is much loved by Victorians. Nothing looks better in an aquarium than a large, gnarled log or tree root, partially buried in the sand. Any wood decoration collected from the wild must be pre-soaked to leach out tannins that will affect the health of the fish in an aquarium.

Leave some open space towards the front of the tank for the fish to swim, and to allow them space to feed. Position the rocks at the back, especially in the corners. This will allow space for territorial males to stake out territories well away from each other.

Vallisneria spp. are a tough group of plants that generally do well in a Victorian tank.

The aquarium should be fairly dark with adequate décor, so that timid fish do not feel overexposed.

AQUARIUM DÉCOR

Wild-collected wood must be soaked before it is placed in the aquarium.

◀ Cork bark.

River wood. ▶

◀ Mopani wood.

AQUARIUM DIMENSIONS

There are very few cichlids that do well in small aquaria, and Victorians are no exception. This is due to their territorial behaviour when adult, and the fact that adult males claim part of the aquarium from which they will expel all other fish except females wanting to breed.

A water volume of 150 litres is the smallest acceptable size. This is equivalent to a size of a conventional three-foot tank (90 x 50 x 40 cm), but half as wide again. An ideal size is the classic four foot (1.2 m), or 200- to 250-litre aquarium. Bigger is always best.

ESSENTIAL EQUIPMENT

The aquarium should be fitted with a tight-fitting hood containing fluorescent lighting. As many Victorians are greenish in coloration, avoid yellow to white light as the aquarium will adopt an unattractive yellowish cast.

Tubes producing blue or violet light give a clear appearance, similar to natural daylight, and also emphasise blue or reddish colours respectively, especially on the fins, as many Victorians have red fins.

Yellow and white lights do not flatter the greenish colour of many Lake Victoria cichlids; blue or violet light is more complimentary.

Light should be turned off at night as cichlids, like many fish, rest at night. The lights should be set to come on after daybreak each day, to prevent the aquarium being subjected to instantaneous full light which will terrify your fish.

One of the reasons that Victorian cichlids look unattractive in dealers' tanks is their ability to lose colour rapidly when stressed. These cichlids *must* have an aquarium that cannot be seen right through, i.e. there should be a suitable background, and sufficient cover in the form of deep caves to enable the fish to find refuge from the light.

Bare glass tanks, or those with just sand and no décor (as in many retail stores), will result in unattractive greyish-green fish with no colour. The more plants, rocks and/or wood, and the larger the aquarium, the better their colours will be displayed.

CHAPTER 4

FEEDING VICTORIA CICHLIDS

Many people ask if their fish will do well on ordinary flake food. To answer this, ask yourself how long you would live on a diet of bread, milk, and an apple a day. You would do fine for several weeks; after that, you would grow heartily sick of it!

Although the manufacturers of artificial feeds often claim them to be 'a complete diet', fish need variety in their diet. Nearly all Lake Victoria cichlids are opportunistic in their feeding, i.e. some species might primarily graze algae from rocks, but should they find an abundance of zooplankton or aquatic insect life, they

Supplementing a diet with live foods helps to keep Lake Victoria cichlids such as this *Haplochromis argens* male in the best health and colour.

Earthworms are a favourite treat for Lake Victoria Cichlids.

will gorge on it. Thus, their captive diet should also be supplemented with live foods wherever possible.

It does not take long to dig a few earthworms from the garden, and if you are taking the trouble to keep these rather exclusive fish anyway, it is worth making the time to keep them healthy and in their best colour.

Most aquarium fish should be fed twice a day, and in this respect Victorian haplochromine cichlids are no different. While in the wild, most are bottom- or mid-water feeders, they soon accept floating food with no problems.

FROZEN LIVE FOODS

There are numerous frozen live foods available which are excellent as supplements (not as staple food), such as various types of small worms, *Daphnia*, *Cyclops*, mosquito larvae, shrimps, and bloodworm.

I have seen several references to the undesirability of frozen bloodworm (sometimes inaccurately called 'red mosquito larvae', though they are, in fact, chironomid midge larvae) as a food for fish. This is because the commercial production of this food is claimed often to take place in polluted waters, which may harbour either heavy metals or parasites harmful to fish.

Frozen live foods are excellent supplements to a flake diet. Pictured: frozen bloodworms, glassworms, brine shrimp and *Daphnia*.

In my experience, I have found little problem with feeding good-quality frozen bloodworms to fish. Most relish this food, and it is ideal for bringing breeders into condition for spawning. Bloodworm should be fed only twice a week, as a supplement to dry foods such as *Spirulina* flake or food granules.

FLAKE FOOD

Many fish foods have too high a protein content (more than 40 per cent protein) for herbivorous species and this may lead to the disease known as 'bloat', which is often a result of intestinal problems.

It is better to feed a lower percentage protein flake or granule (25-35 per cent protein) and supplement occasionally with live food, or frozen live food.

Flake food with a high protein content can lead to health problems.

A healthy, varied diet will keep your fish bright-eyed and in the very best condition.

HUNGRY AND HEALTHY

One day each week, it is good practice not to feed the fish. This is not cruel (they can go many days with no food, and do so in the wild under certain conditions) and will often induce spawning behaviour. At the same time, any uneaten food is found and consumed, which helps water quality. It must be emphasised that, within certain limitations, "a hungry fish is a healthy fish"!

MAMMAL MEAT

Do not feed cichlids from Lake Victoria with frozen ox-heart, or any other type of mammalian meat. They will grow fast, but may soon suffer from all sorts of internal disorders.

The basic diet should be tailored, where possible, to the species' natural diet, with *Spirulina* flake for the herbivores, and a higher protein flake or pellet for piscivores. The most important aspect, to ensure good health, is a varied diet, without too much dried food.

CHAPTER 5

COURTSHIP AND BREEDING

Most of the species are easy to breed and you may find disposal of the numerous young difficult. Victorian cichlids mature at a size of 45 to 55 mm (1.7-2.2 in) standard length (i.e. excluding tail/caudal fin) and an age of six months or more, depending on their growth rate up to the stage of maturity.

When males first adopt their breeding coloration, they will begin to become quarrelsome with each other and stake out territories. However, the instinct for territoriality is not as strong as it is with the mbuna from Malawi, and with several species (*Haplochromis* sp.

Lake Victoria Cichlids are not as territorial as their Malawi counterparts.

The males of some Victoria species, such as the *Haplochromis* sp. 'deep-water', above, should be kept separately to avoid aggressive behaviour

'deepwater' and *H.* sp.' velvet black' are exceptions!) more than one male can be kept if the aquarium is 1.2 metres (4 ft) long (250 litres) or more, with plenty of refuges.

A ratio of one male to four to six females works well, but may be impracticable for the hobbyist, as many retail outlets do not like to stock so many of the drab-coloured females.

Too few females can result in harassed, hollow-bellied and weak females that will not breed well, or survive the rigours of the male's attentions for long.

As far as is known, all Victorian haplochromine cichlids are maternal mouthbrooders (with one possible exception). The male can mate with many females which then carry the fertilised eggs in the buccal cavity (mouth).

Mouthbrooding females seek the refuge of rocks or driftwood shelter to escape further attention from either the male or non-mouthbrooding females.

'Deepwater' male and female. Here the male (right) is exhibiting full breeding coloration.

HATCHING

The eggs hatch after 36-48 hours at 28-30°C, (82-90°F) or 48-72 hours at 24-27°C (74-80°F), depending on the species. They are then carried for a further 12-17 days before the fry are capable of surviving on their own. This does not correlate with the mouthbrooding period in the wild, which for some species may be up to three weeks after spawning.

However, experience with many species of mouthbrooding cichlids in captivity has shown that the fry will often be lost if the females retain them for this long a period in aquaria.

If the aquarium is occupied by other fish, most of the fry will be consumed by the inhabitants after they have been released by the mouthbrooding female. To prevent this, either the mouthbrooding female or her recently released fry should be removed to another aquarium if you want to save the juveniles.

It is important to note that removal before 10 days often results in the female panicking and ejecting the eggs into the catching net.

Astatotilapia latifasciata is a prolific breeder, producing up to 100 fry per brood. Pictured: a male and female.

NUMBER OF YOUNG

The number of young produced per spawning is a function of several factors: species, size, health, food supply and whether the spawning act has been disturbed by other fish.

Certain species seem consistently to produce large spawns, for example *Astatotilapia latifasciata* ('zebra obliquidens') and the well-known *H.* sp. 'thick skin' (also known as *Haplochromis obliquidens* or Species CH44) can produce up to 100 fry per brood. Others, such as the thick-lipped *Haplochromis chilotes*, have smaller spawns of around 15 to 30 juveniles.

FEEDING THE FRY

It is preferable that the free-swimming fry receive food just before their yolk sac is fully absorbed. The yolk sac is clearly visible as a yellowish bulge in the ventral region just posterior to the head. Once this bulge is no longer visible, the yolk sac is absorbed and the juvenile is then dependent on taking in food through its mouth.

In an aquarium occupied by other, non-breeding, fish this can be a problem as all the available food is taken up by these fish, leaving very little for the fry still in the mother's mouth. Her protective instinct will not allow her to release them for fear of the predators around who would rapidly consume them; therefore they become virtual prisoners, starving to death in her mouth once all the yolk is absorbed.

Experience has shown that living fry removed from a mouthbrooding female's mouth, which have not fed subsequent to the absorbtion of the yolk sac, will have very little chance of survival. They will die off over a period of several days even in the presence of suitable food. To prevent this, small quantities of *Artemia* nauplii (newly-hatched brine shrimp) should be added to the tank from 10-12 days after spawning. If this food is not available, one of the dry – or, even better, micro-encapsulated liquid-type – fry foods can be fed.

Commercial hatcheries usually strip the females of fry 10 days post-spawning to maximise juvenile production, but this is not recommended for hobbyists whose aim is to enjoy and observe the natural biological sequences of courtship, spawning, and parental care.

JUVENILE TANK

Only when juveniles have attained about two-thirds of the length of adults should they be introduced to the adult aquarium. Small fry of 20 to 30 mm (0.75-1.25 in) length will be hunted down and eaten by most species.

Even if the juveniles are not eaten, small individuals may be bullied by dominant resident adult males, and cannot hold their own. They should instead have a tank of their own with similar-sized tankmates.

CHAPTER
6

POPULAR CICHLIDS

To illustrate the most commonly available Victorian haplochromine cichlids, six species have been selected and their special needs have been examined.

While other generic names apart from *Haplochromis* (such as *Neochromis*, *Paralabidochromis*, and *Xystichromis*) are sometimes used in scientific circles, these are as yet in a state of flux and I will stick with the names presently established in the hobby.

- *Haplochromis* sp. 'thick skin'
  Also known as Species CH44 and *Haplochromis obliquidens*, although the latter is a different species not yet established in the hobby. Misidentified as *H. brownae* in the aquarium trade
- *Astatotilapia latifasciata*
  The so-called '*zebra obliquidens*' from Lake Nawampasa, also confusingly traded as '*obliquidens*'
- *Haplochromis* sp. 'red head nyererei'
- *Haplochromis* sp. 'crimson tide'
- *Haplochromis* sp. 'flameback'
- *Haplochromis* sp. 'deepwater'.

HAPLOCHROMIS SP. 'THICK SKIN'
H. sp. 'thick skin', together with *Astatotilapia nubila* and *H.* sp. 'flameback' are possibly the most common Victorian cichlids to be found in aquarists' tanks

today. This is because of their dramatic coloration and low price, together with the ease of keeping and breeding them.

There seems to be some doubt as to the geographical origins of this common species, which has been in the aquarium trade for more than 25 years. Possibly the more sandy regions of Lake Victoria were its favoured habitat before the destruction brought about by the Nile perch, but it still appears to be quite widespread around the lake, and is also found on the fringes of rocky areas.

Exporters from several different localities have exported this species over the years and possibly distinct races have been collectively bred together.

A pair of *Haplochromis* sp. 'thick skin'. Note the brighter colours of the male.

COLORATION

Unlike some other Victorian cichlids, male *H*. sp. 'thick skin' retain their dramatic coloration even under sub-optimal conditions, such as overcrowded tanks.

Adult males are brightly coloured with black bars on a yellow background. The fins are red, including the caudal (tail) fin. Immature fish and females are a dull yellowish silver, and can easily be confused with those of other species, such as *H*. sp. 'flameback'.

This is one of the Victorian species that can change its colour dramatically according to mood. When purchased from the fish store, they can completely lose their colour and even males become a dull yellow. However, within minutes of being introduced to a clean, well-planted tank, the males can colour up with jet black barring, and start courting females, if mature.

MATURITY

This species can mature at a very small size (40 mm/1.5 in) and from the age of four months. If they breed at this size in aquaria, the young tend to be few (10-15). Adult females of 55-60 mm (2.2-2.4 in) can produce 45-60 or more fry per spawning. Very large females of 80 mm (3.2 in) can produce more than 100 fry per spawning!

The males are not overly aggressive unless the aquarium is too small, and three to four males can be kept together with females in a tank of 1.2 m (4 ft) or more provided there are plenty of refuges for sub-dominant individuals.

SPECIAL CONSIDERATIONS

H. sp. 'thick skin' makes no special demands of the

aquarist in terms of water quality or food, and may grow larger in captivity than in the wild: males of 110 mms (4.3 ins) being common.

This is one of the most outstanding species to come from Lake Victoria, and deserves a place in any African cichlid collection.

ASTATOTILAPIA LATIFASCIATA

As indicated by its scientific name, and despite its confusing common name (Zebra obliquidens), this cichlid is not closely related to the species above. The name *'obliquidens'* came about due to a superficial resemblance to *H.* sp 'thick skin', despite the fact that *A. latifasciata* comes from a completely different body of water (Lake Nawampasa)!

As with *H.* sp. 'thick skin', this species is well suited to aquarists starting with Victorian cichlids.

Astatotilapia latifasciata is one of the most distinctive of all Lake Victoria basin cichlids.

If males are kept slightly hungry, they show their best coloration — note the bright red flanks on this *Astatotilapia latifasciata*.

COLORATION

A. latifasciata has an advantage over many Victorian species in that the fish show colour from day one. The bold black stripes on a gold background are present even in juvenile fish of 20 mm (0.75 in) in length. Both male and female have this pattern and this makes their identification among other Victoria basin species easy, and hence they can be kept in a mixed species tank.

The black bars on the male are more velvet-black than in females, although the colour of mouth-brooding females does intensify to a deep golden yellow on the flanks.

Males begin to mature at around 50 mm (2 in), at which size they acquire a deep-red patch behind the gill cover. Females never show this red coloration, and thus sexing this species is easy. Males also grow substantially larger than females.

They grow well on a diet of *Spirulina* flake food, with occasional feedings of frozen *Daphnia* and bloodworm.

If feeds are small and the fish are kept slightly hungry, the males show their best colour, with the red markings intensifying to blood red: truly a beautiful sight!

COMPATIBILITY

This is one of the Victoria basin species that does not do well if mixed with Lake Malawi mbuna. The mbuna eventually dominate the *A. latifasciata* to such an extent that they become hollow-bellied and fade away.

However, they mix well with most Victorian species and appreciate slightly softer water and lower pH than most cichlids from Lake Victoria itself (pH 7-7.5, conductivity 150-250 microsiemens).

SPECIAL CONSIDERATIONS

A. latifasciata is one of the species that is least damaging to plants in the aquarium, despite the fact that adult males commonly grow to 120 mms (4.7 ins) in large aquaria.

Its native habitat, Lake Nawampasa, is a small clearwater lake full of aquatic plants; this should be duplicated in the aquarium to bring out the best in this species.

Males are not particularly aggressive with each other, but breeding in the confines of a small aquarium can be problematic: much courtship and pre-spawning activity takes place, but this can be followed up with little to no actual spawning. However, in larger aquaria they are prolific spawners with large broods of more than 100 fry.

An adult pair of *Haplochromis* 'red head nyererei' in breeding colour.
Both sexes show the distinctive black diagonal line through the eye,
so typical of many Victorian haplochromine cichlids.

A. latifasciata is unlikely to hybridise with other
species, but care should nevertheless be taken if other
members of the genus *Astatotilapia* are kept in the same
aquarium.

HAPLOCHROMIS SP. 'RED HEAD NYEREREI'

This species is one of the 23 or so species forming the
H. nyererei species complex. They are true mbipi (and
one of the smallest species), the Victorian analogues of
the mbuna of Lake Malawi, the essentially rock-
dwelling cichlids of that lake, e.g. *Pseudotropheus* and
Melanochromis. Males may grow to 80 mm SL (3 in)
and females to 65 mm (2.5 in).

COLORATION

Immature fish and females are very green in colour,
with a steep upper-head profile. The head of mature
males is covered with red that may extend back over the
chest and flanks, behind the opercula (gill covers). In
breeding colour, the dorsal fin is whitish-blue and the

flanks of the fish have indistinct vertical barring over a golden-green base colour.

As mentioned above, *H.* sp. 'red-head nyererei' is part of a complex of species, many of which have dark coloration with red or orange fins. However, this species differs from the classic 'black-with-red-fins' coloration of so many Victorian male cichlids.

Females of all members of the *H. nyererei* complex generally exhibit a muted version of the male coloration, most having faint vertical barring. Some of the best-coloured forms available to aquarists are:

- *H.* sp. 'nyererei Python Island' (yellow-gold dorsal surface and upper flanks)
- *H.* sp. 'nyererei Makobe Island' (red dorsal surface and upper flanks)
- *H.* sp. 'black and orange nyererei' (black males with yellow fins, from Ndurwa Point)
- *H.* sp. 'zebra nyererei' from Python and Igombe Islands (silver and black striped males with reddish unpaired fins).

To bring out their best colours, they need a staple diet of *Spirulina* flake and occasional feedings of frozen bloodworm or *Daphnia*. However, live foods, such as live mosquito larvae and chopped small earthworms, work wonders for their health and coloration!

I have found that the presence of algae in the aquarium is appreciated by members of this species, who nibble at it.

COMPATIBILITY
Males are intolerant of other mature males, and

although little actual fighting seems to occur (or is actually witnessed by the hobbyist) sub-dominant smaller males are often found dead. The male aggression also extends to females that are immature or unwilling to spawn and which reject the male's courtship.

However, once a stable community has been established, they are a rewarding and colourful species, that will breed well in a large aquarium, if they are the sole occupants. It is best to remove the mouthbrooding female to separate quarters if the brood of fry is to survive.

Females do not tend to spit their young out on netting if the eggs have hatched, unlike *A. latifasciata* which is a classic 'net-egg-spitter'!

This species does not do well with other Victorian species and is best kept in a species tank.

SPECIAL CONSIDERATIONS

Despite its attractive colour, this is one of the lesser-known species from the lake, and tends to be more demanding than the previous two species, as far as husbandry is concerned.

H. sp. 'red head nyererei' demands excellent water quality, with efficient filtration. In the wild, the fish are found only around two islands in the Speke Gulf in the southern part of the lake, and have a restricted distribution. They live in clear water with abundant rocks, and stable water chemistry, and this must be duplicated in the aquarium.

HAPLOCHROMIS SP. 'CRIMSON TIDE'

H. sp. 'crimson tide' is a species closely related to *H.*

nyererei, and has its origins in the northern waters of Lake Victoria. For some reason, this species is less well known than many others, which is unfortunate as it is undemanding in its husbandry, vivid in its coloration, and generally a hardy fish.

'Crimson tide' mature at a length of around 50 mm (2 in), at which size they can begin spawning and produce upwards of 30 juveniles per brood. Large females of 65 mm (2.5 in) may have broods numbering in excess of 60 fry, and have the ability to spawn quite regularly every five to six weeks in the aquarium.

The sex ratio of the offspring tends to be male dominated (around 3:1). Whether this is the result of sibling rivalry at a very early age, resulting in the loss of some of the smaller females, is not yet known.

COLORATION

The coloration is difficult to describe, owing to the variety of colours expressed by different individuals. The most distinctive aspects are the red snout, the prominent dark vertical barring and the bluish-white

The glorious colours of a male *Haplochromis* sp. 'crimson tide' develop early, as in this young male of 65 mm (2.5 in).

dorsal fin. At certain times 'crimson tide' shows lots of red on the fins and flanks.

This species is difficult to confuse with many others as the adult coloration is expressed (albeit more weakly) at an age of just a few weeks and a length of 35-40 mm (1.3-1.5 in).

Large male 'crimson tide' of 80-90 mm (3.2-3.5 in) may be very dark in colour, and tend to lose the vibrant colours of younger fish. Adult females exhibit a muted version of the male coloration, with less distinct barring and red colour on the face and fins, and a greenish cast over the flanks.

SPECIAL CONSIDERATIONS

'Crimson tide' is not particular regarding water chemistry or feeding. A diet of *Spirulina* flake supplemented with twice-weekly additions of bloodworm, *Daphnia*, and/or mosquito larvae is sufficient to keep them in good condition for years. The larger specimens love earthworms, and are quite capable of coping with full-sized worms dropped in whole!

They are an 'intelligent' species and quickly get to know their owner and his feeding routine, and will virtually climb out of the tank at feeding time!

The choice of tank décor for this species is really up to the aquarist, as experience has shown that caves and refuges are rarely used, except by mouthbrooding females and small females escaping the attention of excessively large males.

If the aquarium contains a number of similarly-sized males and females, they tend to spend most of their time in the mid-water region, unlike *H.* sp. 'red-head nyererei' which prefer to be near, or on, the bottom, or hidden in caves.

COMPATIBILITY

Young males are not overly aggressive and three males can be accommodated in a 1.2-m/250-litre (48-inch/62.5 US-gallon) aquarium, together with six to eight females. However, two of the males will become subdominant and lose much of their splendid coloration.

Whilst chasing and mock attacks often take place between males, little physical damage appears to be done, as long as the 'junior' male realises his position in the hierarchy! Older adult males should not be kept together, although several large males (100 mm/4 in) may be kept successfully in very large display tanks without females.

'Crimson tide' can hold their own with most of the other more robust Victorian cichlids, including *H*. sp. 'deepwater', *H*. sp. 'thick skin', and *Astatotilapia nubila*. They are not recommended as suitable for aquaria containing the more docile *H*. sp. 'flameback', *H*. sp. 'red head nyererei', or small *A. latifasciata*.

HAPLOCHROMIS SP. 'FLAMEBACK'

The 'flameback' is the icon of Victorian cichlids, whose picture adorns so many book covers, magazine articles, and posters. The vivid crimson-red dorsal surface is so strikingly different from any other freshwater fish that these cichlids were an instant 'hit' when first made available in the late 1980s.

Regrettably, their specific geographical origin, and suitability for aquaria, are not quite so straightforward.

The 'flameback' is one of the more docile and delicate cichlid species from the Lake Victoria basin. There are at least two superficially similar species that may be sold under this name, one of which originates in Lake Victoria proper, and one from Lake Nawampasa (recently named *H.* sp. 'all red'). It is the former species that is common in the trade.

Males mature at around 50 mm (2 in) in length, while females remain slightly smaller at this stage. Although males can attain 90 mm (3.5 in) in very large aquaria, a more usual maximum size is 75 to 80 mm (2.9-3.2 in), with females much smaller at 55-60 mm (2.2-2.4 in).

COLORATION

'Flameback' males in the wild are crimson-red along the entire dorsal surface and have greenish flanks. However,

'Flameback' adult males show varying amounts of red to plum colour on the dorsal surface, and velvet black pelvic fins.

in captivity, this coloration is often muted, and most particularly the specimens seen in dealers' tanks are a shadow of their real potential. I have seen adult flamebacks in retail outlets that show no red colour at all, to such an extent that it is difficult to distinguish males from females.

Do not be discouraged! This is one of the more timid species that needs the 'protection' of covered or painted rear and side glass panels of the aquarium to make it feel secure.

If kept under the correct conditions – bright light, clean water and suitable tank décor – 'flameback' males can be a stunning sight with their usually crimson, sometimes almost purplish-red, backs.

COMPATIBILITY

Males are only weakly territorial and appear to do little physical damage to each other, so more than one can be kept in an aquarium of 1.2 m/250 litres (48 in/62.5 US gallons).

While the best sex ratio is one male per five to six females, this is impractical for most hobbyists, and one male to two to three females will suffice.

SPECIAL CONSIDERATIONS

'Flamebacks' do not destroy plants, and are at their best in a large, brightly-lit aquarium with a dark, sandy substratum, well planted with *Vallisneria* and other tough plants. Ideally, the corners should contain driftwood or rocks to provide refuges and shelter from the bright lighting.

'Flamebacks' are bottom-loving species and spend their time foraging around the plants for edible debris.

Female 'flamebacks' never show the red colour of the males and are relatively drab. Pictured: a mouthbrooding female.

Breeding requires excellent water quality: an efficient filtration system is a prerequisite, as the water must be totally free of pollutants.

Broods are large with more than 60-80 fry from a large female. The fry are delicate by cichlid standards and require very clean water with regular feedings of *Artemia* nauplii (newly-hatched brine shrimp).

This is one of the species that will retain its fry in the mouth for extended periods if there is a threat of predation. The result is undernourished fry that rarely survive.

Unlike some other mouthbrooding species, the female 'flameback' does not appear to ingest food for the fry while mouthbrooding, and they therefore starve once the yolk sac is absorbed, if the female retains them beyond this period.

Before she is returned to her normal quarters, the female should be conditioned in her own tank for several days to recover from her abstinence of two weeks or so!

HAPLOCHROMIS SP. 'DEEPWATER'

H. sp. 'deepwater' is one of the easiest Victorian species to keep and breed. This is one of the smaller species of rock-dwelling cichlids from Lake Victoria (in aquaria, males do not usually exceed 70 mm (2.75 in) in length and females 55 mm/2.2 in). They are distinctive due to their large heavy head, and large bright ocelli on the anal fin (egg spots).

'Deepwater' come from the southern part of Lake Victoria, primarily the rocky coastline, and are part of a complex of several closely-related species. The species that is usually available for aquaria is the actual *H.* sp. 'deepwater', but there are also *H.* sp. 'yellow deepwater', *H.* sp. 'blue deepwater', and *H.* sp. 'slender deepwater' which have not yet become established in the aquarium trade.

While the name suggests they are found in deep water, this is not quite so, and most are found between 2 and 10 metres (6.5-32.5 ft) of depth, although

H. sp. 'deepwater' is one of the easiest Victorian species to keep and to breed.

usually along steeply sloping rocks that descend much
deeper than this. They are not found in inshore rocky
crevices, nor along sandy or stony beaches.

COLORATION

This is one of the many species from the lake that are
'black-with-red-fins', although a closer examination of
the fish out of water will, in fact, show that they are a
distinctive dark green in colour with a pale blue section
in the spiny part of the dorsal fin.

The sight of a black 'deepwater' displaying his wine-
red fins and tail to a group of females is well worth the
trouble taken to set up the group in the suitable
conditions they need.

Moreover, as they can be kept together with the
yellow-and-black *H.* sp. 'thick skin', and the vertically
barred *H.* sp. 'crimson tide' and *A. latifasciata*, a
community tank of Victorian cichlids is indeed
possible, and colourful to boot!

COMPATIBILITY

Male 'deepwater' are extremely aggressive to individuals
of the same species and will not tolerate another male
in the same aquarium.

Putting two or more males with females in an
aquarium almost always results in the death of the
subdominant male(s), and the females are also so
harrassed that they rapidly lose condition.

However, one male with five to six well-fed females is
usually a recipe for success. While the male is very
attentive to the females, he will not usually physically
damage them, providing that there is plenty of cover in
the form of bogwood or rockwork.

FEEDING

When kept in aquaria, 'deepwater' are, in many ways, very similar to the mbuna of Lake Malawi and like to scrape algae and other organisms off rocky surfaces.

If fed a diet of purely dry foods, they will not show that beautiful velvet-black with wine-red fins, and their diet should be supplemented with bloodworms, mosquito larvae, and *Daphnia*.

In the wild, they appreciate small snails, so if you have a source of the softer planorbid type (ramshorn snails), 'deepwater' will add these to the menu. The spiral-pointed Malaysian sand-burrowing snails are too tough for them to crush, although they may be able to cope with juvenile snails of this type.

BREEDING

As with *H*. sp. 'crimson tide', the progeny of *H*. sp. 'deepwater' seem to be dominated by males. In this case, juvenile aggression is almost certainly the cause, and even 25-mm (one-inch) fry can be very intolerant of each other's company if reared in too small a tank.

The juveniles (30-60 per brood) are hardy from day one and can easily be reared on powdered dry foods without the need for live *Artemia* nauplii. This ease of breeding and rearing has meant that this attractive Victorian is one of the most widely available and reasonably priced Lake Victoria cichlids around.

Males colour up to their adult black colour at a very small size (40 mm/1.5 in), although females are always a drab greenish grey. Because of this, the examples usually available in retail outlets are often purely sub-adult males which already show adult coloration, and are therefore attractive to purchasers. Females, being

smaller and so drab in colour, are often rejected by
store-owners as being 'slow-movers', unattractive to the
uninformed aquarist.

If females are available, it is best to purchase five
times as many females as males and take the smallest
male available: this will give the females a chance to
become established and strong enough to survive the
ardour of the male's passion.

Alternatively, if no breeding is desired, buy purely
males as their aggression is strongest in the presence of
females. 'Target fish' in the form of the other Victorian
cichlids mentioned above are highly recommended with
this species, as they divert the attention of over-active
males from harrassing the females.

It is unwise to keep *H*. sp. 'velvet black' with *H*. sp.
'deepwater', owing to their similar appearance,
especially the close similarity of the females.

An adult female 'deepwater' – the yellow colour on the fins and
chest intensifies during courtship.

SPECIAL CONSIDERATIONS

'Deepwater' can be quite destructive of plants and only the best-rooted, tough ones will survive its excavations and manic desire to rearrange the tank décor to its own liking! As with *H.* sp. 'thick skin', *A. latifasciata*, and *H.* sp. 'crimson tide' (all suitable tankmates), they make no special demands regarding water quality.

It has often been shown that aggression increases with temperature; therefore, a temperature maintained at 22 to 24°C (71-75°F) is adequate to keep them healthy and cool the ardour of the males at the same time.

Breeding will still take place at these temperatures, but lethal aggression is less than at such elevated temperatures as 26 to 29°C (78-84°F).

HELPFUL HINTS

This section comprises anecdotal information that has been gleaned from keeping and breeding Victorian cichlids for many years. As with all such information, these are personal experiences that may work well under certain conditions but cannot be accepted as hard-and-fast rules for all aquaria in all situations.

However, assuming that the reader is keeping, or intending to keep, these cichlids to try something new, and is a reasonably experienced aquarist, then he/she will understand the vagaries of keeping fish, especially that most irrational of single-minded beasts: the cichlid!

Generally, cichlids from different parts of the world should not be kept together – but there are exceptions. The Malawi *Labidochromis caeruleus* (pictured) mixes well with many other peaceful African mouthbrooders.

Haplochromis chilotes is a peaceful fish that requires quiet, non-aggressive tankmates.

WHAT FISH CAN I KEEP WITH VICTORIAN CICHLIDS?

Essentially, none. I feel that, if an aquarist has progressed to the point of wanting to try Lake Victoria cichlids, he/she will have passed the stage of wanting to mix species from different parts of the world together in one aquarium. But realistically, we cannot, and

---

Victorian cichlids that should be kept in a species tank or with peaceful tankmates

H. piceatus (black with red fins)

H. sp. 'flameback' (red dorsal surface)

H. sp. 'red head nyererei' (red head, green body)

H. chilotes (thick lips, bluish-green body with red flash)

H. sp. 'orange rock hunter' (orange coloured piscivore: eats small fry and juvenile fish)

should not, all be purists, and indeed the hobby would be a dull one if we were! So, here's a brief list of African cichlid species that I have found to work *reasonably* well together, either collectively (as in 1, below), or individually (as in 2-5, below).

	Victorian species	Suitable Lake Malawi species	Suitable other African cichlids
1	*H.* sp. 'deepwater'	*Aulonocara* spp.	*Astatotilapia burtoni*
	H. sp. 'crimson tide'	*Labidochromis caeruleus*	*Pseudocrenilabrus philander*
	H. sp. 'thick skin'	*Pseudotropheus demasoni*	*Astatotilapia calliptera*
	A. latifasciata	*Pseudotropheus saulosi*	
	H. nigricans	*Cynotilapia afra*	
	H. sp. 'scraper'		
	H. sp. 'blue obliquidens'		
	A. nubila		
2	*H.* sp. 'flameback'	*Aulonocara* spp.	
3	*H.* sp. 'red head nyererei'	*Labidochromis caeruleus*	
4	*A. latifasciata*	*Copadichromis* spp. *Mylochromis* spp. *Aulonocara* spp.	
5	*A. nubila*	Various Malawi mbuna	

HOW CAN I STOP MY CICHLIDS FROM KILLING EACH OTHER?

With aggressive species, keep only one male per harem of females. With the more gentle species, keep three or more males: if two males are kept in a single aquarium, the dominant male will always persecute the other.

Females should always have plenty of cover. A clay flowerpot with a mouth diameter of 10-12 cm (4 in), partially buried in the gravel and with its entrance semi-blocked by rocks, works well. Alternatively, use twisted wood roots reaching almost up to the surface, or floating cork bark: harrassed females often hang at the surface to escape the attention of the male.

Never add new females to an established aquarium during daylight, leave it until the lights are turned off, or remove the male and return him later. It is never a good idea to add just one new fish at a time: rather, add several to spread the aggression.

A dominant male can make life miserable for other males in an aquarium. Pictured: an unhappy-looking *H*. sp. 'flameback' male.

CAN I KEEP THE LIGHTS ON ALL THE TIME?

No, cichlids need to rest just the same as any other animal, and 24-hour light would be most unnatural! About half an hour after turning off the lights, you will see most of the fish resting on or near the bottom. They cannot close their eyes as they have no eyelids. Fish undoubtedly rest and take some time to 'wake up' if suddenly plunged into full light from total darkness.

The best system is a timer switch that automatically turns the lights off before the house lights go off, and comes on after daybreak. This will simulate dawn and dusk, and will prevent the fish being shocked by being suddenly plunged into light or total darkness, which would be very unnatural.

Bare, brightly-lit tanks are stressful to fish. Even in a well-decorated tank, fish need rest from the light. Pictured: *Psammochromis riponianus*.

Echinodorus (above) and *Cryptocoryne* (right) species are both suitable for a Victorian aquarium.

CAN I KEEP PLANTS IN A LAKE VICTORIA AQUARIUM?

In general, these cichlids are less damaging to plants than Lake Malawi mbuna.

Lake Victoria has abundant rooted aquatic vegetation in the shallower regions, although this has been much reduced by the spread of water lettuce (*Pistia stratiotes*) and, more particularly, water hyacinth (*Eichornia*

POPULAR LAKE VICTORIA BASIN CICHLIDS

SCIENTIFIC NAME	COMMON NAME
H. sp. 'thick skin'	Obliquidens
H. nigricans	Nigricans
H. sp. 'copper black'	Copper black
H. sp. 'crimson tide'	Crimson tide
H. chilotes	Thick lips
H. sp. 'red head nyererei'	
H. sp. 'black and orange nyererei'	
H. sp. 'zebra nyererei'	
H. sp. 'emerald fire'	Emerald fire
H. sp. 'deepwater'	Deepwater
H. sp. 'velvet black'	Velvet black
H. argens	
H. limax	Limax
H. sp. 'Hippo Point'	Hippo Point salmon
H. sp. 'rock kribensis'	Rock kribensis
H. piceatus	
H. sauvagei	Migori sheller
H. sp. 'orange rock hunter'	
H. phytophagus	Christmas fulu
H. sp. 'dayglow'	Dayglow fulu
Astatotilapia latifasciata	Zebra obliquidens
A. nubila	Haplochromis Nubilus
Astatoreochromis alluaudi	
Astatotilapia brownae	

AVAILABLE TO THE HOBBY

PLACE OF ORIGIN

Northern Lake Victoria

Widespread in Lake Victoria

Widespread in Lake Victoria

Northern Lake Victoria

Widespread in Lake Victoria

Speke Gulf, Lake Victoria

Speke Gulf, Lake Victoria

Widespread in Lake Victoria

Lake George

Mwanza and Speke Gulfs

Widespread in Lake Victoria

Possibly extinct in Lake Victoria

Lake George

Hippo Point, Lake Victoria

Widespread in Lake Victoria

Possibly extinct in Lake Victoria

Widespread in Lake Victoria

Mwanza Gulf, Lake Victoria

Lake Kanyaboli / Yala swamp

L. Kanyaboli /Yala swamp

Lake Nawampasa

Lakes Victoria/ Kyoga/Nabugabo

Widespread in Victoria basin

Southern Lake Victoria

crassipes), in recent years as the lake water has become enriched with nutrients through human activities. Some of the peripheral or 'satellite' lakes, such as Lake Nawampasa, have very clear water with abundant emergent (rising above the water's surface) and submerged aquatic vegetation.

In general, the best aquatic plants to use are *Vallisneria* (both straight leaf and spiral 'vallis'), Amazon swordplants (*Echinodorus* spp.), Java moss (*Vesicularia dubyana*), and some of the more robust *Cryptocoryne* species. These are all readily available and will not break the bank if the fish turns rogue and digs them up or turns them into salad against all the rules!

Plants should be either planted in pots, with the pot section buried in the gravel, or securely surrounded by small pebbles that will discourage the cichlids from disturbing them.

Lake Victoria Cichlids must be provided with adequate cover to feel happy and secure. Pictured: *Haplochromis argens*.